To You, My Friend,

I wish to give you a gift—
Something you might not give yourself.
To lift your spirit and refresh you.
To encourage and cheer your heart.
You say you've never enough of it.
Although I can't give you a year,
or a month,
or a week.
I'd like to give you a moment—
A moment to take time . . .

With Love,

TAKE TIME

A

MOMENT

for the

HEART

by Melody Carlson

0-8054-2359-1

Published by Broadman & Holman Publishers
Nashville, Tennessee
Cover & Interior Design: Koechel Peterson & Associates,
Minneapolis, Minnesota

Dewy Decimal Classification: 242
Subject Heading: Meditations
Library of Congress Card Catalog Number: 99-087149

Unless otherwise indicatd all Scripture references
are from the New King James Version (NKJV),
copyright ©1979, 1980, 1982, 1990
by Thomas Nelson, Inc. Publishers.

Library of Congress Cataloging-in-Publication Data
Carlson, Melody.
    Take time : a moment for the heart / Melody Carlson.
        p. cm.
    ISBN 0-8054-2359-1
    1. Christian women—Prayer-books and devotions—English.
        2. Meditations. I. Title.
BV4844.C32   2000
242'.643—dc21

99-087149
CIP

1 2 3 4 5   04 03 02 01 00

Dedication

For Carol Jean Schmidt

I encourage you (once again) to take time to

nurture your soul.

With love,

Melody

To everything there is a season, A time for every purpose under heaven.

ECCLESIASTES 3:1

Foreword

Most of us feel pressed for time. We hurry through our days, trying to accomplish more than may be humanly possible. Often, we rush so fast, we barely notice as our days turn into weeks . . . weeks into months . . . and before we know it we feel frazzled and old. We wonder where the time has gone.

This book is an open invitation to *slow down*—if only for a moment—to *take time* to experience the fullness of life and living with all of your senses tuned in. It's a gentle but urgent reminder to *stop and smell the roses*. While it's unlikely that everyone will do *all* the moments in this book, I encourage you to do as many as you can— and to be thoroughly refreshed in the process. So whether you do one moment a day—or one moment a week—I hope you'll be inspired to view time differently and to fully experience the beauty of life with each new day.

Blessings,

Melody Carlson

Breathe Deeply

How often we partially hold in our breath, almost as if we're afraid to completely inhale; or perhaps we're just waiting to exhale. Do we fear there's insufficient air for all, or do we believe we're conserving energy? Whatever the cause, it makes no sense. Our lungs were designed to *breathe*—to breathe deeply! Fresh oxygen relaxes, refreshes, and actually sustains our bodies. It even enhances our ability to think, reason, and create. So why do we deny ourselves such a simple pleasure?

Sit back in your chair, shoulders squared. Take a moment to exhale . . . and then breathe in deeply, slowly. Hold the air in your lungs for a brief moment and then exhale slowly again. Repeat this for several moments, allowing your entire body the luxury of relaxation and refreshment. It's so simple. And yet we forget.

The LORD God formed man...and breathed into his nostrils the breath of life; and man became a living being.

GENESIS 2:7

I take pleasure in infirmities....For when I am weak, then I am strong.

2 CORINTHIANS 12:10

Forgive Yourself—for Not Being Perfect

We all long for perfection—some of us more than others. Yet that longing is a human quality that's meant to remind us of our deep and never-ending need for God and His infinite perfection. Often, however, we turn this longing against ourselves, falling into the frustrating trap of *perfectionism,* placing impossible demands on our lives. We expect to do all, be all, have all. Then when we fail, we are disappointed. And, oh, do we fail!

TAKE A MOMENT TO FORGIVE YOURSELF FOR FAILING AT PERFECTION. ADMIT THAT YOU'RE NOT PERFECT. NEVER WILL BE! ACCEPT THAT GOD DESIGNED US TO BE IMPERFECT, AND THAT ONLY BY HIS TOUCH WILL WE BE PERFECTED. REALIZE THAT OUR IMPERFECTION CAN BE AN ENDEARING HUMAN QUALITY THAT MAKES US APPROACHABLE AND REAL TO OTHERS.

Remember a
Happy Time from Childhood

Sometimes we become so busy being grown-up that we almost forget that we were once children. Yet if we are honest with ourselves, we must admit that buried beneath our layers of maturity and experience lives that same little child from years gone past. Certainly there may be some old hurts and disappointments, but there are some successes and joyful moments too. By acknowledging and even celebrating that child within us, we become better equipped to face the life ahead.

Take a moment to remember a delicious slice of childhood. Perhaps it was a sunny day at the beach when a sand castle came out just right, or the first time you made it to the top of that cherry tree. Allow yourself to savor the memory, to delight in the simple pleasures of childhood. Then take a piece of that joy back into adulthood with you.

Jesus called a little child to Him ... "Unless you ... become as little children, you will by no means enter the kingdom heaven. ... whoever humbles himself as this little child is the greatest in the kingdom of heaven."

MATTHEW 18:2–4

Truly the light is sweet,

And it is pleasant for the

eyes to behold the sun.

ECCLESIASTES 11:7

TAKE TIME TO

Admire a Sunset

It's the end of the day, and we're usually in a hurry—chauffeuring tired kids home from sports practice, planning dinner, trying to finish that over-due report, or thinking about getting that last load of laundry folded. We might snatch a glance at a rose-colored sky from the rearview mirror as we try to pass that slow-moving truck up ahead, but who has time to actually stop and watch the sun set? And then again, who has time *not* to?

TAKE A MOMENT TO SLOW DOWN, PAUSING TO ADMIRE THE SIGHT OF THE SUN SINKING INTO THE WESTERN HORIZON. REMEMBER THAT IT WAS IN THE "COOL OF THE EVENING" THAT GOD CAME INTO THE GARDEN OF EDEN TO STROLL WITH ADAM AND EVE. RECOGNIZE THAT THIS IS A DELICATE TIME OF DAY—A MOMENT FOR PEACE AND REFLECTION—AND REVEL IN IT.

TAKE TIME TO

Reach Out to a Child

Why is it that some adults appear to think children are less significant than their grown-up counter-parts? Is it because they are smaller, younger, and not able to drive cars or earn a living? All these reasons seem ridiculous, and yet there are times when we all fall victim to this sort of mentality. After all, children can be loud and annoying; they get dirty and break things. But then . . . so do adults.

TAKE A MOMENT TO SEE A CHILD WITH NEW EYES. (REMEMBER HOW YOU FELT WHEN, AS A CHILD, YOU WERE TREATED AS IF YOU WERE INVISIBLE.) REACH OUT TO A CHILD NEAR YOU—PERHAPS A RELATIVE, A FRIEND, A STRANGER. SEE IF YOU CAN CATCH A GLIMPSE INTO A CHILD'S SOUL. PREPARE TO BE AMAZED!

But Jesus said,
"Let the little children come to
Me, and do not forbid them; for of
such is the kingdom of heaven."

MATTHEW 19:14

Rest in the LORD,

and wait patiently for Him.

PSALM 37:7

Sit in a Rocking Chair

Aren't rocking chairs just for old people? For those who have the leisure time to sit on a wide verandah sipping iced tea? No one really lives that kind of life, do they? Besides, think of all that energy wasted while you simply rock back and forth, over and over, without *getting anywhere!* But wait a minute. Can you recall any warm memories associated with a rocking chair? How about the time you sat on Grandma's lap and listened to a story? Or the times you rocked your own sweet babe back to sleep in the wee hours of the morning?

TAKE A MOMENT TO SIT IN A ROCKING CHAIR. THEN, ROCKING SLOWLY BACK AND FORTH, ALLOW THE GENTLE RHYTHM TO SOOTHE YOU AND LULL YOU INTO A PLEASANT MEMORY OF TIMES GONE BY. SIMPLY RELAX AND ENJOY THE PLEASANT REPETITION OF THE MOVEMENT, ALLOWING TODAY'S CARES TO SLIP AWAY LIKE WATER FLOWING OVER A STONE.

Experience a Small Piece of Nature

In Japanese culture there is great respect for the most basic elements of nature. Perhaps this is the result of too many people living in too little space; but nonetheless, the Japanese enjoy an appreciation that we Westerners often miss. In Japan they might celebrate the simple beauty of a single leaf, a cherry blossom, or a smooth stone. And yet we, often surrounded by some of God's most beautiful creation, forget to pause and take notice.

Take a moment to study the simple beauty of a flower or leaf. Notice the graceful shape, the intricacies of the veins that have given it nourishment and life. Feel the velvety smoothness of a rose petal; smell the fresh, pungent fragrance of a pine needle. Develop the art of appreciation.

Consider the lilies of the field, how they grow.

MATTHEW 6:28

"Oh, that I had wings like a dove!
I would fly away and be at rest."

PSALM 55:6

Watch a Bird in Flight

Have you ever noticed how birds are almost everywhere? Even in the heart of a bustling city you'll find flocks of pigeons gathered in hopes of finding leftover lunch morsels. Usually we notice these creatures when they're on the ground, and sometimes we lament the messes they make and consider them a general nuisance. We fail to appreciate their amazing aeronautical design and the way they gracefully lift themselves to the sky and soar above the busyness below.

TAKE A MOMENT TO WATCH A BIRD IN FLIGHT. SEE HOW IT SPREADS ITS WINGS AND FLOATS ON THE UPDRAFTS AS IF IT HASN'T A CARE IN THE WORLD. APPRECIATE ITS FREEDOM, ITS GRACE, ITS SWEET ABANDON. THEN ALLOW YOUR SPIRIT TO DO THE SAME, TAKING A MOMENT TO SOAR ABOVE THE COMPLEXITIES OF DAILY LIFE.

Reflect upon a Day When You Felt Special

The problem with life is that it is so *daily*. One day blends into the next, and an entire week can pass without anything seemingly significant occurring. Sometimes it seems it's part of the human condition to fall victim to the humdrum of the everyday—the doldrums of daily life. We tend to forget that there was ever a day when it was any different. However we've all had days when we've accomplished something worth celebrating. Unfortunately we quickly forget them and move on, sometimes even neglecting to celebrate them at all.

TAKE A MOMENT TO REMEMBER A DAY WHEN YOU FELT TRULY SPECIAL. PERHAPS IT WAS AN ACADEMIC ACHIEVEMENT, OR A PERSONAL VICTORY, OR EVEN YOUR WEDDING DAY. ALLOW YOURSELF TO RELIVE THAT HAPPY MOMENT—AND TO CELEBRATE IT ONCE AGAIN.

I remember the days of old;

I meditate on all Your works.

PSALM 143:5

But the LORD made the

heavens. Honor and

majesty are before Him;

Strength and beauty are in

His sanctuary.

PSALM 96:5–6

Praise God for Creation

Sometimes we can become almost intimidated with the idea of celebrating the incredible beauty of nature—as if to acknowledge the wonders of this physical world might somehow detract from God's glory. How completely ridiculous! Do we honestly believe that to admire a majestic old oak we might be mistaken for pagan tree worshipers? Or that to marvel at a snowcapped mountain might in some way rock God from His throne? Don't we realize that nature is the very workmanship of God's own hands? To celebrate creation is to praise our mighty Creator!

TAKE A MOMENT TO REALLY SEE AND EXPERIENCE A PART OF GOD'S WONDERFUL CREATION—WHETHER IT'S A CLOUD-SWEPT SKY, A GRASSY MEADOW, OR A GNARLED OLD TREE. THEN ALLOW YOURSELF TO BE MOVED AND TOUCHED BY ITS BEAUTY, AND PRAISE GOD FOR BEING THE MIGHTY CREATOR OF SUCH GLORIOUS WONDERS.

Say "I Love You"

We all know that actions speak louder than words. We also know that words can be hollow and empty if they're not spoken from the heart. But sometimes we use these principles (true as they may be) as excuses to shy away from speaking the actual words. We assume that others will know that we love them when we fix them a meal, do an unexpected favor, or give a gift. While these actions are all valuable, often they cannot equal the power of three simple words said in earnest.

TAKE A MOMENT TO TELL SOMEONE THAT YOU LOVE THEM. MAKE A PHONE CALL, WRITE A NOTE, OR SIMPLY WHISPER IT IN THEIR EAR. NOTICE HOW YOUR HEART FEELS AS THIS TRUTH ESCAPES YOUR LIPS. AND REMEMBER, YOU DON'T ALWAYS GET A SECOND CHANCE TO SAY SUCH THINGS OUT LOUD.

"By this all will know that you
are My disciples,
if you have love for one another."

John 13:35

They shall still bear fruit in
old age; They shall be fresh
and flourishing.

PSALM 92:14

Listen to an Elderly Person

We live in a culture where youth is blatantly worshiped. Middle-aged baby boomers spend billions of dollars on ways to avoid wrinkles and sags and graying hair—as if growing old is a curse to be avoided at all cost. Yet who can escape it? What's more, have we considered how this attitude must make an elderly person feel? Have you ever noticed how some people tend to avoid looking at an elderly person on the street, as if afraid that aging is a contagious disease? Yet what many of the elderly do have is the kind of wisdom that's only acquired through years of living. How much we will lose if we forget to listen.

TAKE A MOMENT TO LISTEN TO AN ELDERLY PERSON. YOU MAY BE SURPRISED AT HOW EAGER THEY ARE TO BE HEARD, AND HOW THEY OFTEN FEEL INVISIBLE IN TODAY'S CULTURE. LOOK INTO THEIR FADED EYES AND CONSIDER ALL THAT THEY HAVE SEEN AND EXPERIENCED. LEARN FROM THEM..

Relax in God's Grace

The world pushes in on us from all angles. Daily assaults from the media urge us to be more efficient; to drive faster cars; to invest in higher-earning markets; to be better dressed, better looking, even better smelling! To listen and heed all this brouhaha is to try harder and harder, until we gradually succumb to the thinking that we will never be good enough. But God's grace is not like that. God's grace is *sufficient*. What's more, He bids us to come just as we are.

TAKE A MOMENT TO CONSIDER GOD'S GRACE IN YOUR LIFE—HOW HE FREELY GIVES IT, EXPECTING NOTHING IN RETURN. NOW, SIMPLY RELAX. ALLOW YOURSELF TO SINK INTO GOD'S GRACE JUST AS YOU WOULD SINK INTO A SOFT FEATHER MATTRESS. REST IN HIS GRACE

For it is good that the heart
be established by grace...

HEBREWS 13:9

For with the heart one believes unto righteousness, and with the mouth confession is made unto salvation.

ROMANS 10:10

Share a Secret Desire

Sometimes we become so caught up in the demands of daily living that we think our only desire is for the next light to turn green or to get a good night's sleep. It's easy to forget the dreams of our youth, the unfulfilled desires of our heart. We simply move on, putting one weary foot in front of the other, asking ourselves, *What difference would it make now?* Perhaps the very idea of actually verbalizing a secret desire sounds scary and somewhat humiliating. Sometimes, however, it is only when we voice our hidden dreams that they begin to sprout wings.

TAKE A MOMENT TO CONSIDER VOICING A SECRET DESIRE TO SOMEONE YOU LOVE AND TRUST, SOMEONE WHO CARES DEEPLY ABOUT YOU, SOMEONE WHO WON'T LAUGH. IF YOU FEEL THERE'S NO SUCH PERSON IN YOUR LIFE RIGHT NOW, REMEMBER THAT GOD IS LISTENING— AND HE LONGS TO GIVE YOU THE DESIRE OF YOUR HEART.

TAKE TIME TO

Think Good Thoughts

It seems the world bombards us with negativity at every turn. Daily, the newspaper blasts out every manner of bad news, often with a twist that makes it sound worse than it really is. The hottest media topics seem to be the ones about heartbreak, betrayal, or loss. Also, have you ever noticed how bad news travels at least twice as fast as good? Unfortunately, it seems to be part of the human condition. But God encourages us to rise above it.

TAKE A MOMENT TO FOCUS ON SOMETHING THAT IS TRULY GOOD. MAYBE IT'S A RELATIONSHIP, A PLEASANT EVENT, OR AN UNEXPECTED FAVOR. IMAGINE WAYS THAT A SITUATION MIGHT IMPROVE. CONSIDER HOW SOMEONE YOU LOVE MIGHT SUCCEED IN A CERTAIN AREA. REALIZE THAT THERE IS A POWER IN THINKING POSITIVELY.

Whatever things are true, whatever things are noble, whatever things are just, whatever things are pure, whatever things are lovely, whatever things are of good report, if there is any virtue and if there is anything praiseworthy — meditate on these things.

PHILIPPIANS 4:8

"*For if you forgive men their trespasses, your heavenly Father will also forgive you.*"

MATTHEW 6:14

Forgive an Old Hurt (Again)

We've all been hurt, some of us more than others. Hopefully we've forgiven those who've hurt us, but we seldom forget the incidents, do we? That old saying, "Forgive and forget," only seems to work for those who've suffered amnesia or a lobotomy. The rest of us tend to remember. And sometimes we repress those memories without realizing that we need to forgive again. Perhaps that's one reason Jesus said to forgive seven times seventy.

TAKE A MOMENT TO ASK YOURSELF IF YOU ARE HARBOR- ING A TINY SEED OF UNFORGIVENESS IN YOUR HEART. IS THERE SOMEONE YOU'VE FORGIVEN, BUT NEED TO FORGIVE AGAIN? TAKE THIS MOMENT TO ACKNOWLEDGE THAT YOU FORGIVE HIM OR HER. ASK GOD TO GRACE YOU WITH THE ABILITY TO FREELY FORGIVE.

TAKE TIME TO
Enjoy God's Creatures

Have you ever considered that we are outnumbered on this earth? By animals! Certainly there are those that seem pesky, like mosquitoes and fruit flies and long-tailed rodents. But do you ever wonder if God had something more in mind when He created all those incredible creatures? Pets are easy to enjoy; we can appreciate their unconditional loyalty and devotion, and even laugh at their antics. But what about the rest of the animal kingdom? Is there something we're missing?

TAKE A MOMENT TO APPRECIATE GOD'S CREATURES. WHETHER IT'S TO ADMIRE A HIGH-STEPPING HORSE OR A WELL-TRAINED DOG; OR TO STROKE THE SOFT, FURRY COAT OF A PURRING CAT; OR EVEN TO OBSERVE AN INDUSTRIOUS SPIDER SPINNING AN INTRICATE WEB. TAKE TIME TO SEE WHAT ANIMALS CAN OFFER, EVEN IF IT'S SIMPLY A GOOD LAUGH AT THE MIMICKING CHIMP IN THE ZOO.

Go to the ant.... Consider her ways
and be wise, Which, having no captain,
Overseer or ruler, Provides her
supplies in the summer, And gathers
her food in the harvest.

PROVERBS 6:6–8

Then the Lord spoke to Moses...
"From everyone who gives it
willingly with his heart you shall
take My offering....oil for the
light, and spices for the anointing
oil and for the sweet incense...."

Exodus 25:2–6

Enjoy Pleasing Aromas

Some people think that the only reason we have a sense of smell is to protect us from dangers, like when we smell smoke and sense fire nearby, or when we notice a putrid smell and know that food is rancid. But if that's true, then why can we also enjoy pleasant aromas—things like a spicy pumpkin pie, the sunny fragrance of lavender, or a pungent pine bough? Undeniably, God created our noses for more than just safety purposes. As we look through the Old Testament, we see numerous references to fragrant incenses that are a pleasing offering unto God.

TAKE A MOMENT TO FOCUS ON THE SCENTS AROUND YOU. CONSIDER WHICH FRAGRANCES BRING PLEASURE AND THEN INCORPORATE THEM INTO YOUR WORLD (THROUGH CANDLES, POTPOURRI, SCENTED OILS, ETC.). LEARN TO APPRECIATE AND ENJOY NATURAL AROMAS— A RAINY DAY, FRESH-BAKED COOKIES, EVERGREENS, AND SO MUCH MORE.

Take an Imaginary Retreat

For those of us lucky enough to get a vacation, we may discover that a once-a-year retreat can quickly turn into a hectic and frantic attempt to do and see all. When we return home (feeling frazzled and exhausted and anything but refreshed) we find that we need a vacation just to recover from our vacation. Perhaps by midwinter we may even be asking ourselves, "Is that all there is?" But God, the great Creator, has imparted us with creativity. It's possible to use our imaginations to take us temporarily away from the grind of the day.

TAKE A MOMENT TO IMAGINE AN EXOTIC PLACE YOU'D LIKE TO BE—A SUNNY, DESERTED ISLAND; A CABIN IN THE MOUNTAINS; A SAILBOAT ON THE CARIBBEAN; OR EVEN HEAVEN. THEN IMAGINE THAT YOU ARE THERE— SMELL THE TREES, HEAR THE LAPPING WATER, FEEL THE WARM SUN. FINALLY, RETURN REFRESHED.

Thus says the LORD:
"Heaven is My throne, And
earth is My footstool. Where
is the house that you will build
Me? And where is the place of
My rest? For all those things
My hand has made, And all
those things exist."

ISAIAH 66:1–2

When He established the clouds above,...He strengthened the fountains of the deep.

PROVERBS 8:28

Look for Formations in the Clouds

Usually when we look up at the clouds, we're trying to decide whether or not we'll need sun-block or an umbrella. Even though we look, we don't often see. But can you remember a lazy day of childhood, when flat on your back you gazed up into the clouds to spy a elephant with trunk held high, or a leaping bunny with long, floppy ears? Who has time for such childish pursuits these days? Consider terminally ill patients and how they know their time is very limited. Yet many would happily take time to spot a kangaroo hopping across the sky.

TAKE A MOMENT TO GAZE UP AT THE SKY. RELAX AND GET COMFORTABLE AS YOU ALLOW YOUR EYES TO EXPLORE THE HEAVENS. DELIGHT IN SPOTTING A FIRE-BREATHING DRAGON, A GALLOPING HORSE WITH FLOWING MANE, OR ANY OTHER WONDER THAT MAY BE HIDDEN THERE.

TAKE TIME TO
Breathe a Prayer

Sometimes when we think about praying, we envision a long, drawn-out process of going off by ourselves, kneeling down and reverently bowing our heads, and then speaking beautifully worded prayers. While that's certainly not a bad practice, it isn't always possible or even practical. The truth is, most of us lead busy and demanding lives with little time to go off into seclusion for great lengths of time. Yet, we *know* we need to pray. And often!

HOW TO BREATHE A PRAYER: FIRST, DIRECT YOUR THOUGHTS TOWARD GOD. THEN TAKE A DEEP BREATH AND HOLD IT FOR A MOMENT WHILE YOUR SPIRIT FOCUSES ON GOD. SLOWLY EXHALE AS YOU FORM A SIGNIFICANT WORD/REQUEST IN YOUR MIND (LOVE, THANKS, FORGIVENESS, MERCY, BLESSING, ETC.). REPEAT AS NECESSARY.

Pray without ceasing...

1 Thessalonians 5:17

Giving thanks always for all things to God the Father in the name of our Lord Jesus Christ.

EPHESIANS 5:20

Give Thanks

It's easy to find something to complain about: bad weather, an unappreciative boss, snarled morning traffic, corruption in government—the list goes on. And if *we* don't complain, we know that someone else surely will! But the funny thing is, singing the complainin' blues almost never makes us feel better. If we're honest, we'll admit that it's a hard habit to break. Besides that, we know how God delights in thankful hearts. Now, how do we get there?

TAKE A MOMENT TO PRACTICE THANKFULNESS. START WITH ONE THING THAT YOU'RE TRULY THANKFUL FOR. PERHAPS IT'S YOUR CHILD'S HEALTH, OR A DEPENDABLE FRIEND, OR A SUNNY DAY. THEN REALIZE IT'S A GIFT FROM GOD, AND EXPRESS YOUR SINCERE THANKS..

Recall a Time When Someone Helped You

Sometimes it feels as if nobody cares. We plod along doing our daily chores, facing life's little challenges and trying to do our best even when no one is watching. But sometimes the day grows long and weary, and we feel very much alone. It can seem as if everything we've ever accomplished has been through our own efforts, with no help from anyone. Yet if we examine our hearts, we must admit that there have been those who've assisted us along the way.

TAKE A MOMENT TO RECALL A TIME WHEN SOMEONE LENT A HELPING HAND. PERHAPS IT WAS DONE IN SECRET. OR SIMPLY IN PASSING. PERHAPS IT CHANGED YOUR ENTIRE LIFE. ALLOW YOURSELF TO EXPERIENCE THE WARMTH OF GRATITUDE AS YOU FONDLY REMEMBER THIS PERSON'S KINDNESS

Give thanks to God always for you....remembering without ceasing your work of faith, labor of love, and patience of hope in our Lord Jesus Christ in the sight of our God and Father.

1 Thessalonians 1:2–3

Nothing is better for a man
than that he should eat and
drink, and that his soul should
enjoy good in his labor.

ECCLESIASTES 2:24

Take Time to
Taste Something New

How easy it is to get into a rut—especially with something as daily as food. How many times have you repeated the same menu: toast, juice, and coffee for breakfast; yogurt and fruit for lunch; something easy for dinner (or perhaps pizza delivery again)? We encourage our children to try new things, but how often do we take our own advice? How many times have you barely glanced at the menu before ordering the "tried and true" at your favorite restaurant? Sometimes we *need* to take a risk, and tasting something new is a relatively small one.

TAKE A MOMENT TO TASTE SOMETHING NEW—PERHAPS SOMETHING FROM ANOTHER CULTURE, OR SOMETHING FAMILIAR COOKED IN A NEW WAY. SURE, IT'S POSSIBLE YOU MIGHT NOT LIKE IT, BUT EVEN THAT IS A SENSATION WORTH EXPERIENCING. WHO KNOWS, YOU MIGHT ACTUALLY LOVE IT!

TAKE TIME TO

Listen

Sounds are all around us. Sometimes the cacophony grows so persistent that we long for escape. We may learn to tune the noise out, or we grow accustomed to certain sounds and no longer consciously hear them. Occasionally we become comfortable with background noise, and we think we cannot live without a TV or radio playing wherever we go. Unfortunately, one result of constant exposure to all these noises is that we forget how to really listen.

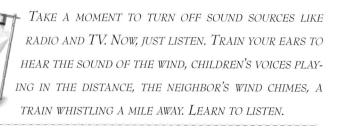

TAKE A MOMENT TO TURN OFF SOUND SOURCES LIKE RADIO AND TV. NOW, JUST LISTEN. TRAIN YOUR EARS TO HEAR THE SOUND OF THE WIND, CHILDREN'S VOICES PLAYING IN THE DISTANCE, THE NEIGHBOR'S WIND CHIMES, A TRAIN WHISTLING A MILE AWAY. LEARN TO LISTEN.

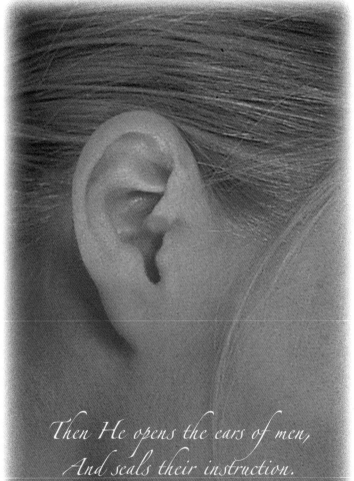

Then He opens the ears of men,
And seals their instruction.

JOB 33:16

Be still, and know

that I am God.

PSALM 46:10

TAKE TIME TO
Be Still

We live in a fast-paced culture where to "do nothing" is often seen as laziness. Performance-oriented achievers frown upon the man who sits quietly on the park bench for longer than it takes to tie a shoelace. Some people think it's a waste of time to read a whole book. And when someone asks what we've been up to, we often feel compelled to give a detailed activity report, wrapping it up with how we are so pressed for time! When did it become shameful or slothful to *not* be "too busy"?

Take a moment to do absolutely nothing. Allow yourself to relax, empty your thoughts, and be still. Don't be surprised if it's not easy, but don't give up. Just breathe deeply, relax, and be still. Then once you are still, remember that God is God.

TAKE TIME TO

Count Your Blessings

Did your grandma ever say, "You better count your blessings!"—almost as if it was an admonition or warning? Or maybe you've heard of people who count their blessings to lull themselves to sleep— like counting sheep. But perhaps you think if you tried to count yours, you'd be stuck by blessing number two. The truth is, if we open our eyes, we can find all kinds of blessings, both big and small, in and about our lives. Many we take for granted; some we ignore; others we may have forgotten.

TAKE A MOMENT TO CONSIDER HOW ABUNDANTLY GOD HAS BLESSED YOU. START WITH SIMPLE THINGS LIKE EYES OR FEET, THEN WORK YOUR WAY UP TO THINGS LIKE FOOD, HOMES, PETS, CHILDREN, RELATIONSHIPS, PEACE. PERHAPS EVEN MAKE A LIST. THEN THANK GOD FOR EACH THING YOU CAN THINK OF.

Enter into His gates with thanksgiving, And into His courts with praise. Be thankful to Him, and bless His name. For the LORD is good; His mercy is everlasting, And His truth endures to all generations.

PSALM 100:4–5

And I appeal to you...bear with the word of exhortation, for I have written to you in few words.

HEBREWS 13:22

Write a Letter

In this highly evolved age of technology, we've come to rely on things like phones, faxes, voice mail, and E-mail to communicate with each other. Some people fear letter writing may soon be a lost art. Yet how comforting and therapeutic it can be both to write and receive a thoughtful, hand-written letter from a loved one. Something happens when we take a good pen and begin to slow ourselves down enough to etch our thoughts onto the surface of a fine piece of stationery.

TAKE A MOMENT TO CONSIDER SOMEONE YOU'D LIKE TO ENCOURAGE WITH A HAND-WRITTEN MESSAGE, THEN GATHER THE APPROPRIATE TOOLS INTO A QUIET SPACE AND ALLOW YOURSELF THE TIME TO THINK AND TO WRITE. DO NOT STRIVE FOR PERFECTION, BUT RATHER FOR HEARTFELT COMMUNICATION.

Express Your Love to God

Surely God *knows* that we love Him. After all, He can see deep inside of us and read the secrets written upon our hearts. Doesn't it sound slightly trivial to say "I love you" to God—the Almighty, the Creator of the universe? It's not like He's on some ego trip and needs to hear us going on about how much we love Him. But perhaps it isn't so much for God's ears as it is for our hearts. Perhaps we need to tell God we love Him as a reminder to ourselves that it is so. Besides, does a father ever tire of hearing that his children love him?

TAKE A MOMENT TO COME BEFORE YOUR HEAVENLY FATHER WITH AN HONEST AND OPEN HEART. CONSIDER HOW MUCH HE LOVES YOU, HOW HE WOULD GATHER YOU INTO HIS LOVING ARM, HOW HE HOLDS YOU IN THE PALM OF HIS PROTECTIVE HAND. THEN EXPRESS TO HIM HOW MUCH YOU LOVE HIM.

I will love You,

Oh LORD,

my strength.

PSALM 18:1

Praise the LORD with the harp;
Make melody to Him….Sing to
Him a new song; Play skillfully
with a shout of joy.

PSALM 33:2–3

TAKE TIME TO

Sing Out Loud

OK, so maybe you can't carry a tune in a bucket, and you wouldn't dare sing out loud in public. But the booming sales of tapes and CDs certainly says most of us enjoy music. The question is, have we turned into a nation of listeners only? Don't we remember how to sing along? It's important to note that *singing is healthy*. It's good for the mind, the body, and the spirit.

 *TAKE A MOMENT TO SING, REALLY SING. YOU CAN TUNE IN THE RADIO, POP IN A TAPE, OR WING IT ON YOUR OWN. BUT GO AHEAD AND SING. SING WITH GUSTO! AND WHEN YOU'RE DONE, OBSERVE HOW SINGING OUT LOUD CHANGES YOU.*

TAKE TIME TO

Listen to Your Heart

Sometimes it seems we're constantly listening to voices, both big and small. "The dog chewed on my soccer shoes ... he ate the last bowl of Crunchios... can you drop these by the cleaners..." and on the chatter goes. Amazingly we adapt ourselves, even learning how to sift out some of the less significant prattle. But sometimes in the process of tuning things out we inadvertently tune out our own hearts. When was the last time you really listened to your heart? Not some motivational speaker or your best friend's analysis of how to fix your life, *but your own heart.*

TAKE A MOMENT TO FIND A SECLUDED SPOT, FREE FROM DISTRACTION. THEN QUIET YOUR MIND. BREATHE DEEPLY AND RELAX. THEN LISTEN. WHAT IS YOUR HEART SAYING? PERHAPS IT WON'T BE CLEAR AT FIRST, BUT KEEP LISTENING UNTIL YOU KNOW.

'Trust in the LORD with all your heart, And lean not on your own understanding; In all your ways acknowledge Him, And He shall direct your paths.

PROVERBS 3:5–6

Then David danced
before the LORD
with all his might.

2 SAMUEL 6:14

TAKE TIME TO
Dance All Alone

Have you ever watched a beautiful ballet, the rhythmic steps of Riverdance, or even John Travolta discoing in a seventies flick and suddenly felt that little toe-tapping urge to get up and dance? Naturally, you remained firmly planted in your chair. Heaven forbid that anyone should actually witness a mature grown-up dancing in a theater or concert hall. And yet, what about when you're all alone and the music beckons? No one is watching—it's just you and God.

TAKE A MOMENT TO PUT ON THAT SPECIAL KIND OF MUSIC—THE KIND THAT MAKES YOU FEEL LIKE DANCING. THEN GET UP AND MOVE. ALLOW YOUR ARMS AND LEGS TO FREELY RESPOND TO THE RHYTHM AND SOUND. DANCE, DANCE, DANCE!

Write a Poem

Don't you have to take some sort of class to create *real* poetry? Don't poets have to dress weirdly or wear strange jewelry, use strange words or talk funny? Besides, what could a "nonwriting" person possibly have to say in a poem anyway? Not to mention that they wouldn't even know where to begin. Yet, one of the best things about poetry is its ability to free up words. Without the constriction of perfectly formed sentences, the writer is free to express feelings through random and colorful words—and it doesn't even have to rhyme!

TAKE A MOMENT TO CLEAR YOUR THOUGHTS. THEN BEGIN TO JOT DOWN WORDS AND PHRASES THAT ARE LOOSELY FLOATING INSIDE YOUR MIND. PERHAPS THE WORDS DON'T EVEN MAKE SENSE RIGHT NOW. GO AHEAD AND WRITE ANYWAY. NO ONE WILL EVER HAVE TO READ THIS BUT YOU. SIMPLY ALLOW YOURSELF THE FREEDOM OF EXPRESSION.

The heavens declare the glory of God; ...Day unto day utters speech, And night unto night reveals knowledge. There is no speech nor language Where their voice is not heard. ...through all the earth, And their words to the end of the world.

PSALM 19:1–4

"Ask, and it will be given you; seek, and you will find; knock, and it will be opened to you."

MATTHEW 7:7

Daydream

Do you ever remember being chastised as a child for daydreaming? As if to ramble around in one's mind was the most hideous waste of time. Perhaps that is why few adults ever take time to daydream. But consider the great minds throughout history: people like Mozart, da Vinci, Einstein, Edison. What might we have missed out on if they had believed that daydreaming was a waste of time!

TAKE A MOMENT TO DAYDREAM. PERHAPS IT'S A SIMPLE DREAM, LIKE PLANNING YOUR GARDEN OR YOUR NEXT VACATION. OR MAYBE IT'S SOMETHING BIGGER, LIKE A NEW RELATIONSHIP, A JOB CHANGE, OR EVEN A SPIRITUAL REVELATION! GO AHEAD—ALLOW YOURSELF TO DREAM.

Laugh

Although most of us will admit that humor is good for us, it's amazing how many times we attempt to avoid it. We carefully step aside when we see it coming our way, as if it's somehow immature or less than spiritual to laugh too hard or too loud. Certainly daily life can be a sobering experience—just listen to the evening news or your neighbor's latest heartbreak. It's enough to wipe a smile off any face. Still, we desperately need to laugh. In fact, it is healthy to laugh!

TAKE A MOMENT TO SEEK OUT HUMOR IN LIFE. PERHAPS IT'S BY READING A SILLY E-MAIL, RENTING AN OLD JERRY LEWIS MOVIE, OR GETTING TOGETHER WITH SOME LIGHTHEARTED FRIENDS. ALLOW YOURSELF TO BE IMMERSED IN SOME SORT OF HUMOR, AND THEN LAUGH. LAUGH LOUD AND HARD. SEE IF YOU DON'T FEEL BETTER.

Then our mouth was filled
with laughter And our tongue
with singing...

PSALM 126:2

Be anxious for nothing,

but in everything by prayer and sup-

plication, with thanksgiving, let your

requests be made known to God.

PHILIPPIANS 4:6

Take Time to
Pray Out Loud

Sometimes it's hard to pray at all, and praying out loud seems nearly impossible, especially when we're in the thick of a trial and feel as if we've acquired some sort of spiritual lock jaw. Besides, we may not be gifted with a rich vocabulary or a beautiful voice. The mere idea of speaking to God *out loud* makes us feel inadequate and even silly. Nonetheless, sometimes praying out loud is exactly what we need. We need to hear ourselves cry out to God for help, healing, deliverance. We need to hear ourselves simply thanking God and giving Him praise.

TAKE A MOMENT TO FIND A QUIET PLACE; EVEN A CLOSET WILL DO. GET COMFORTABLE, AND CLEAR OUT THE CLUTTER OF THOUGHTS THAT DISTRACT. THEN FOCUS YOUR MIND ON GOD AND BEGIN TO SPEAK OUT LOUD. YOU MIGHT START WITH A SIMPLE PHRASE, LIKE "HEAVENLY FATHER, PLEASE HELP ME."

Visit a Good Bookstore or Library

Most of us know where a good bookstore or library is located. We might pass one regularly as we rush from one of life's demands to the next. Perhaps we even promise ourselves that we'll stop in sometime—*sometime* when life slows down a little and we have time to pick up a good book. Months go by, however, and *sometime* never comes. Oh, what we miss! Books can open up whole new worlds, expanding our everyday lives in ways we cannot imagine. They take us on travels, introduce us to interesting people, and teach us about new things. They enrich our lives.

TAKE A MOMENT TO GO IN A BOOKSTORE OR LIBRARY. REMIND YOURSELF THAT THIS IS SUPPOSED TO BE A TREAT, SO DON'T RUSH YOUR VISIT. ALLOW YOURSELF TIME TO BROWSE. ENJOY THE AROMA AND TEXTURE OF THE BOOKS. GO AHEAD AND READ SNIPPETS. HOPEFULLY SOMETHING INTERESTING WILL WHET YOUR READING APPETITE.

When wisdom enters your heart, And knowledge is pleasant to your soul, Discretion will preserve you; Understanding will keep you.

PROVERBS 2:10–11

Therefore...put on tender mercies, kindness, humility, meekness....

COLOSSIANS 3:12

TAKE TIME TO

Smile at a Stranger

Sometimes it's hard to smile at the people we know, let alone a perfect stranger. Besides, aren't we supposed to be suspicious of strangers? Shouldn't we just keep our eyes straight forward with serious expressions on our faces so we don't encourage any unwanted attention? But consider the people out there who may need a smile—the old, the young, the handicapped, the homeless. So many people feel invisible because passersby avoid eye contact. No one smiles at them. A smile is such a small thing— an inexpensive gift we can give. Its worth, however, is immeasurable.

TAKE A MOMENT TO ASK GOD TO SHOW YOU WHO MIGHT NEED A SMILE TODAY, THEN LOOK DIRECTLY INTO THEIR EYES AND SMILE. THEY MAY BE TOO SURPRISED TO EVEN RETURN YOUR SMILE, BUT DON'T WORRY—THEY WILL REMEMBER IT.

Read a Poem or Scripture Out Loud

We live in an age where many old pleasures are becoming a lost art. Things like storytelling, poetry reading, and extemporaneous speaking are being steadily replaced by various forms of electronic entertainment. Yet we can be deeply touched by hearing a live human voice reciting a lovely poem or reading Scripture. Surprisingly, it can be just as moving to read aloud a poem or Scripture yourself. Speaking and hearing the words somehow helps us to understand them on a whole new level.

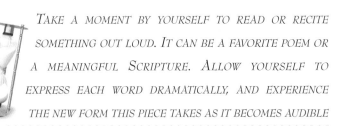

TAKE A MOMENT BY YOURSELF TO READ OR RECITE SOMETHING OUT LOUD. IT CAN BE A FAVORITE POEM OR A MEANINGFUL SCRIPTURE. ALLOW YOURSELF TO EXPRESS EACH WORD DRAMATICALLY, AND EXPERIENCE THE NEW FORM THIS PIECE TAKES AS IT BECOMES AUDIBLE

Let the words of my mouth and the meditation of my heart Be acceptable in Your sight, O LORD, my strength and my Redeemer.

Psalm 19:14

A present is a precious
stone in the eyes of its
possessor; Wherever he
turns, he prospers.

PROVERBS 17:8

Give a Gift for No Reason

We all enjoy giving and receiving gifts from time to time. Yet sometimes, especially at Christmas, the gift process can become overwhelming and burdensome. By the time the new year rolls around you never want to buy or return another gift—ever! But think for a moment; have you ever received a totally unexpected gift, right out of the blue, for absolutely no reason? If you're lucky enough to say yes, remember how that gift made you feel so very special. You have the power to delight someone else with that same kind of pleasure.

TAKE A MOMENT TO CONSIDER SOMEONE YOU COULD BLESS WITH AN UNEXPECTED GIFT. PERHAPS IT'S SOMEONE WHO'S HURTING, OR LONELY, OR JUST BLUE. MAYBE IT'S A GOOD FRIEND THAT YOU'D LIKE TO SHOW SOME APPRECIATION. TAKE THE TIME TO FIND OR MAKE SOMETHING THAT YOU KNOW WILL MAKE THAT PERSON SMILE. AND BEFORE YOU KNOW IT, YOU'LL BE SMILING TOO!

TAKE TIME TO

Create Something Unique

Who has time these days to actually "create" something? Even if you could find the time, would you even know where to begin? Besides, isn't it easier to go out and buy some handcrafted item already made by someone else? Yet, if we're honest with ourselves, we might admit that there's a little place inside us that *longs* to create—even if we don't know quite how. It's because God, the Creator, made us like Himself. Therefore let's look at creativity from a new light and embrace it as part of ourselves.

SEARCH FOR A WAY TO EXPRESS YOUR CREATIVITY. PERHAPS IT'S TO PLAN A SPECIAL MEAL, TO ARRANGE DRIED FLOWERS, OR TO PAINT YOUR BATHROOM PERIWINKLE BLUE! OR MAYBE IT'S TO DOODLE ON A DESK PAD OR WRITE A LIMERICK. WHATEVER FORM IT TAKES, ALLOW YOUR CREATIVITY THE CHANCE TO SURFACE.

And we labor, working with our own hands.

1 CORINTHIANS 4:12

A merry heart makes a cheerful countenance, But by sorrow of the heart the spirit is broken.

PROVERBS 15:13

Tell a Joke

Some days it seems that absolutely nothing in life is very funny. We become so focused on the grim and the negative that we become humorless and gray ourselves. Yet these are the times when we could most use a good laugh. If we look hard enough, we might even spy the lighter side of what at first glance appears to be a somber situation. Perhaps we can recall a funny story or joke that helps us to stop taking life so seriously.

TAKE A MOMENT TO REMEMBER OR FIND A FUNNY JOKE OR STORY (THINGS LIKE Reader's Digest OR YOUR LATEST E-MAIL CAN PROVIDE GOOD MATERIAL). THEN GO AHEAD AND SHARE THIS GEM WITH SOMEONE ELSE. GIVE YOURSELF PERMISSION TO BE A LITTLE BIT SILLY, TO ENJOY SOME LEVITY. REMEMBER, THE BIBLE SAYS GOOD HUMOR IS "HEALTH TO THE BONES."

TAKE TIME TO

Pray for a Stranger

Sometimes it's hard enough to pray for the people
we know and love, let alone pray for a complete
stranger. Yet if we give it a chance, we might be
pleasantly surprised—not only because we find out
it's *possible* to pray for a stranger, but also because
we see how this very act enriches our prayer life. So
often we think we must pray with specific knowledge, asking for the things we assume someone else
desperately needs. But when we pray for a total
stranger, we learn to depend on faith to lead us—
relying on our hearts instead of our heads.

ASK GOD TO SHOW YOU SOMEONE TO PRAY FOR
TODAY. THEN ASK HIM TO GUIDE YOU AS YOU
PRAY—USING YOUR HEART, NOT YOUR HEAD. IT ONLY
TAKES A MOMENT, BUT IT COULD CHANGE A LIFE—
EVEN YOUR OWN.

For we do not know what we should pray for...but the Spirit Himself makes intercession for us with groanings which cannot be uttered.

ROMANS 8:26

"Seek out a man who is a skillful player on the harp. And it shall be that he will play...and you shall be well."

1 Samuel 16:16

Listen to Good Music

There's no disputing that music is good for us.
Some medical researchers have discovered that it
even enhances physical healing. Most of us listen to
music off and on during the day. Sometimes it's
bits of radio, a cassette hastily shoved into the car's
stereo system, or even elevator music. But we often
forget to take time to expose ourselves to the kind
of music that moves us deeply. We get so busy that
we neglect to give ourselves a restful moment with a
favorite selection of classical music, opera, gospel,
jazz, or whatever style specifically restores and
refreshes our souls.

*TAKE TIME TO EXPERIENCE THE TYPE OF MUSIC THAT
SPEAKS TO THE DEPTHS OF YOUR SOUL. ALLOW YOUR-
SELF AN UNDISTURBED MOMENT (ONE SONG OR AN
ENTIRE ALBUM) TO BECOME IMMERSED IN THE BLENDING
SOUNDS, LOST IN THE MELODY, WASHED BY THE BEAUTY.
AND EMERGE REFRESHED.*

Hold Someone's Hand

If you have small children, holding a little one's hand may be an everyday part of your normal routine. Unfortunately, many busy parents are often so distracted that they don't fully appreciate the pleasure of these limited and fleeting moments. Likewise, some of us hold hands with our spouse from time to time in a movie, on a walk, or during a heart-to-heart talk. These moments are also priceless. We need to watch for those times when family members or others we know need encouragement, consolation, or comfort—times when the simply gesture of holding a hand can minister far more than words.

TAKE A MOMENT TO REALLY HOLD SOMEONE'S HAND. PERHAPS IT WILL BE WITH YOUR CHILD OR SPOUSE, AN ELDERLY GRANDMOTHER, OR A FRIEND IN NEED. APPRECIATE THE TEXTURE AND WARMTH OF THEIR HANDS. ENJOY THE CONNECTION, AND FEEL THE ENCOURAGEMENT FLOW.

And our hope for you is steadfast,
because we know that as you are
partakers of the sufferings, so also
you will partake of the consolation.

2 CORINTHIAN 1:7

"Comfort, yes, comfort My people!" Says your God.

ISAIAH 40:1

TAKE TIME TO

Hug Someone

We all need our space. Some of us seem to need more than others. We discreetly keep people at bay—just beyond that invisible line that borders our comfort zone. There are those times, however, when we need to knock down the barriers and reach out for one another. We need to remember that we are all human—and often in need of a human touch. Still, it's not always easy to step out of our comfort zone or to intrude into someone else's space. But when we do, it's almost always worthwhile.

TAKE A MOMENT TO RECOGNIZE SOMEONE IN YOUR LIFE WHO IS IN NEED OF A HUMAN TOUCH. OF COURSE, IT'S ALWAYS EASIER TO RESPOND TO A CHILD OR SPOUSE, BUT PERHAPS THE PERSON IN NEED IS A COWORKER WHO'S HAVING A BAD DAY, A LONELY NEIGHBOR, OR AN ELDERLY FRIEND. REACH OUT AND SHARE A HUG.

TAKE TIME TO

Listen to God

How often our minds race ahead. We make plans,
form mental lists, rehearse words we want to say, or
replay ones we wish we hadn't. Sometimes it seems
that the hullabaloo inside our head is more constant
and distracting than a three-ring circus. That's when
we forget how to be quiet. We neglect to listen to
that still, small voice that belongs to the Creator of
the universe—that voice that speaks words of love
and encouragement to us. We don't always realize
that listening to God takes conscious effort on our
part, requiring great self-control, and the ability to
hush our own random thoughts.

*TAKE A MOMENT TO QUIET YOUR MIND AND FOCUS IN
ON GOD'S PRESENCE. TO CLEAR YOUR THOUGHTS, MED-
ITATE ON A SHORT PHRASE LIKE: "GOD IS LOVE." THEN
ASK GOD TO HELP YOU DEVELOP YOUR SPIRITUAL EARS.
RELAX AND LISTEN TO YOUR FATHER.*

"Come here, and hear the words of the LORD...By this you shall know that the living God is among you."

JOSHUA 3:9–10

The flowers appear on the earth;
The time of singing has come.

SONG OF SOLOMON 2:12

TAKE TIME TO
Arrange Fresh Flowers

Everyone likes to receive a pretty bouquet from time to time. Unfortunately, the occasions seem few and far apart. While we may pass a flower stand or florist shop and even pause to admire the color-ful blooms, we may feel too guilty or undeserving to indulge in such an extravagance for ourselves. We wouldn't think twice, though, about sending an arrangement to someone else. Yet, if we're to love ourselves as we love others, why wouldn't we give ourselves a gift of flowers?

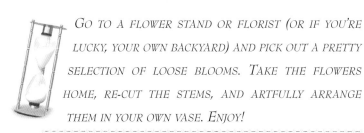

GO TO A FLOWER STAND OR FLORIST (OR IF YOU'RE LUCKY, YOUR OWN BACKYARD) AND PICK OUT A PRETTY SELECTION OF LOOSE BLOOMS. TAKE THE FLOWERS HOME, RE-CUT THE STEMS, AND ARTFULLY ARRANGE THEM IN YOUR OWN VASE. ENJOY!

Receive God's Love

Sometimes we're better at giving than receiving. Receiving makes us uncomfortable, as if by the mere act we suddenly incur some sort of debt, or perhaps we simply feel unworthy. Sometimes this reluctance to receive is unconsciously carried over into our relationship with God. The fact is, God delights to give us good things. Above all, the most precious thing He gives us is His perfect and unconditional love. Yet how often we fold our arms tightly across our chests and stubbornly shake our heads, unable to receive that which we so desperately need.

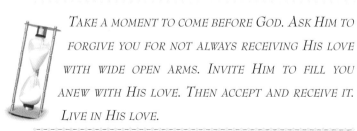

TAKE A MOMENT TO COME BEFORE GOD. ASK HIM TO FORGIVE YOU FOR NOT ALWAYS RECEIVING HIS LOVE WITH WIDE OPEN ARMS. INVITE HIM TO FILL YOU ANEW WITH HIS LOVE. THEN ACCEPT AND RECEIVE IT. LIVE IN HIS LOVE.

We love Him

because He first loved us.

1 JOHN 4:19

Trust in the Lord, and do good; Dwell in the land, and feed on His faithfulness. Commit your way to the Lord, Trust also in Him, And He shall bring it to pass.

PSALM 37:3, 5

Trust God's Provision

The materialistic culture in which we live may actually be driven by a very real need to provide. Parents work long and hard to provide food, housing, clothing, and education for their families. Every day we're bombarded with advertisements and campaigns that urge us to provide in bigger, better, and more expensive ways—often with the help of a credit card. If we succumb to this thinking, we soon begin to feel like caged squirrels running faster and faster on a stationary wheel, the whole time getting nowhere quickly. All this just because of our need to provide.

TAKE A MOMENT TO REMEMBER THAT GOD IS THE GREAT PROVIDER. ALLOW YOURSELF TO RELAX AND TRUST IN HIS ABILITY TO GIVE YOU AND YOUR FAMILY WHAT YOU TRULY NEED. ASK HIM TO SHOW YOU WAYS TO TRUST MORE FULLY IN HIS PROVISION.

Enjoy a Luxurious Bath

Does it feel as if our culture is speeding up on a daily basis, each day moving faster than the previous one? Increased demands and less time equals more frustration and stress. How can we control it? We can't add more minutes to the day, but perhaps we can add more pleasure to the minutes. Choose to *step away* from the chaotic, frenzied pace and step into a world where time seems to stand still. That world can be as close as your bathtub. Cares amazingly slip away within the comforting confines of an uninterrupted, warm, and fragrant bath.

MAKE ROOM IN YOUR BUSY EVENING FOR AN UNDISTURBED BATH. FILL THE TUB WITH WARM WATER AND A DELICIOUS-SMELLING BATH PRODUCT; ARRANGE LIGHTED CANDLES NEARBY; PLAY RELAXING MUSIC; AND FULLY INDULGE YOUR SENSES. EMERGE REFRESHED AND RENEWED.

"Let a little water be brought,
and wash your feet, and rest
yourselves under the tree."

GENESIS 18:4

And do not be conformed to this world, but be transformed by the renewing of your mind, that you may prove what is that good and acceptable and perfect will of God.

ROMANS 12:2

Browse through an Antique Shop or Museum

Living in a modern-day world with modern-day pressures, we sometimes forget the generations of those who have gone before us. As a result, we fail to appreciate a sense of history that can adjust and enhance our current perspective. Taking the time to remember how the pioneers struggled to survive can be a therapeutic reminder of what's really important in life today. Examining old tools, clothing, and furniture can make us thankful for some of our modern conveniences. Observing how life was simpler in the past can be good reminder to slow down.

PLAN A SHORT TRIP TO A LOCAL ANTIQUE SHOP OR MUSEUM. TAKE TIME TO CONSIDER WHAT LIFE WAS LIKE FOR THE PEOPLE WHO ONCE USED THE ITEMS ON DISPLAY. BE REMINDED OF THE TEMPORAL LENGTH OF YOUR EARTHLY LIFE. THEN FOCUS ON WAYS TO MAKE YOUR DAYS MORE SIGNIFICANT.

TAKE TIME TO

Celebrate God's Mercy

We're always looking for reasons to celebrate because celebration is good for the soul. However, instead of waiting for birthdays or anniversaries, why not celebrate something we can experience on a daily basis—like the fact that God's mercies are new every morning. Sometimes we forget what that really means; consequently, we aren't as merciful with ourselves or others as we might be. Yet if we fully embrace God's forgiveness and celebrate His mercy, it can't help but overflow into all areas of our lives, blessing others along the way.

TAKE A MOMENT TO THANK GOD FOR FORGIVING YOU. REALIZE HOW HOPELESS YOUR LIFE WOULD BE WITHOUT HIS GRACE. ALLOW YOUR HEART TO REJOICE AS YOU CELEBRATE ANEW HIS MERCY.

"But with everlasting kindness
I will have mercy on you,"
Says the LORD, your
Redeemer.

ISAIAH 54:8

Delight yourself also in the LORD, And He shall give you the desires of your heart.

PSALM 37:4

TAKE TIME TO

Dream a Big Dream

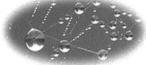

When we were young, we sometimes allowed ourselves to dream really big dreams. Back then, we believed we could do anything, be anything, go anywhere. But as we grew older, we assumed adult responsibilities and settled into our daily routines. As a result, we may have quit dreaming altogether. Maybe we simply buried our dreams so deeply that we think they're dead and gone. Could it be that they are only dormant, like fallen seeds, just waiting for a ray of sunlight to warm them back to life.

TAKE A MOMENT TO REMEMBER AN OLD DREAM—OR DREAM A NEW ONE. WHAT DOES YOUR HEART LONG FOR? DO YOU HAVE A HIDDEN TALENT LYING DORMANT? WHAT WOULD YOU REALLY LOVE TO DO? HOW COULD YOU IMPLEMENT YOUR DREAM? ASK GOD TO HELP YOU WITH YOUR DREAM.

TAKE TIME TO
Call an Old Friend

Some friendships seem destined to live forever. Even when left untended for long periods of time, they always seem to pick up right where they left off. Unfortunately, that may encourage us to take them for granted. But like anything of value, good friendships require attention, maintenance, and an investment of time and energy. How can we enjoy the benefits of a good friendship if we neglect to participate in it?

TAKE A MOMENT TO CALL AN OLD FRIEND. TAKE TIME TO REALLY HEAR HOW SHE'S DOING—THE GOOD AND THE BAD. THEN SHARE LIKEWISE WITH HER. ENCOURAGE HER, AND LET HER KNOW HOW MUCH HER FRIENDSHIP MEANS TO YOU.

For God is not unjust to forget your work and labor of love which you have shown toward His name, in that you have ministered to the saints, and do minister.

HEBREWS 6:10

Let the lowly brother glory in his exaltation.

JAMES 1:9

Celebrate a Past Success

Sometimes when we encounter a triumph or success, we get so caught up in the moment that we almost forget to really *experience* it. Often there's much going on—pats on the back, congratulations—and life momentarily spins into fast speed. Before we know it, it's all over and we're back at the same old grind, our success all but forgotten. Sadly, whether we realize it or not, we've shortchanged ourselves. We need to remember our past successes. We need to acknowledge that we truly accomplished something. We need to celebrate our past triumphs and look forward to future ones.

TAKE A MOMENT TO REMEMBER A TIME WHEN YOU SUCCEEDED AT SOMETHING. RELIVE THE SATISFACTION OF A JOB WELL DONE. THEN CELEBRATE THAT MOMENT ALL OVER AGAIN, ALLOWING YOURSELF TO SAVOR THE PLEASURE EVEN MORE FULLY THAN BEFORE.

TAKE TIME TO

Watch a Sunrise

Sometimes it seems as if morning comes too early. Longing for just a few more minutes of sleep, we don't usually leap out of bed, eager to face the brand new day. In fact, when was the last time you actually saw a sunrise? Are you missing something important? Have you ever noticed how the birds zealously greet the sun each day, singing their happy little songs at the first sign of light? What is it that makes them do that? What can we learn from them?

Decide to rise early and witness a sunrise for yourself. Enjoy the quiet solitude, the delicate sense of hopefulness, the beauty of light chasing away darkness. Be reminded that God is in control. He keeps the earth rotating, the planets in their order. He can also keep you.

He appointed the moon for seasons;
The sun knows its going down.

PSALM 104:19

"But when you do a charitable deed, do not let your left hand know what your right hand is doing, that your charitable deed may be in secret."

MATTHEW 6:3–4

Do a Secret Good Deed

In a cynical world, it's hard for many to believe that anyone ever does anything purely for the goodness of doing it. Most people expect rewards, acknowledgment, or even a raise when they go above and beyond the call of duty. To *secretly* do something out of the kindness of the heart is almost unheard of. But when it happens, people stop and take notice. It reminds us that true benevolence still exists. It gives us hope. And when we do a secret good deed ourselves, it changes our hearts in ways that nothing else can.

Look around and ask God to inspire you to find someone who may be in need of a secret good deed. Then covertly plan a strategy to accomplish the task without revealing your efforts to anyone. Finally, take delight in your mission accomplished.

TAKE TIME TO

Remember You Are God's Child

Sometimes it seems that if only we'd been born into a different situation, our lives would be much better. Fantasies of belonging to a wealthy or famous family, perhaps even royalty, appear the solution for all our troubles. (Of course, we don't consider the challenges that people in those situations must face.) What we tend to forget is that we *do* belong to a royal family. We are the children of the King of all creation. Our Father is God Almighty, ruler of the entire universe! What more could we desire?

TAKE A MOMENT TO REMEMBER WHO GOD IS—HIS OMNIPOTENCE, HIS NEVER-ENDING LOVE, HIS MAJESTY. THEN REMIND YOURSELF THAT HE IS YOUR FATHER. YOU ARE HIS CHILD. WHO CAN CARE FOR YOU BETTER THAN GOD? REST IN THIS KNOWLEDGE.

But as many as received Him, to them He gave the right to become children of God, to those who believe in His name.

JOHN 1:12

But the meek shall inherit the earth,

And shall delight themselves in the

abundance of peace.

PSALM 37:11

TAKE TIME TO

Enjoy a Good Cup of Tea

Americans drink coffee, or so it seems. Oftentimes we get our coffee *to go* because we're on the run. The British, on the other hand, understand how to take time for tea. *Tea* is much more than a drink, it is an event—a time to relax, reflect, and be refreshed. While it's unlikely that we'll all adopt the tradition of afternoon tea, it wouldn't hurt to incorporate a "tea time" into our busy lives at least once in a while. And who knows after that?

PLAN AN AFTERNOON TEA TIME. INVITE SOMEONE TO JOIN YOU. SELECT ONE OF THE MANY AVAILABLE TEAS AND BREW ACCORDING TO INSTRUCTIONS (LOOSE TEA AND TEAPOTS ARE BEST). MAKE SURE TO DRINK YOUR TEA FROM A NICE CUP, AND HAVE SOME SORT OF TREAT TO GO WITH IT. THEN RELAX AND ENJOY!

Reminisce

Don't we have to be old to reminisce? Who has time for such things anyway? It's more than enough just to keep up with life's daily demands as we work to build new memories for ourselves and our families. We can reminisce later. Yet there are things we can learn as we reflect on and embrace our past. Remembering events in our childhood, both good and bad, can help us to understand why we do the things we do as adults. It can make us better parents, companions, people.

TAKE A MOMENT TO REFLECT ON SOMETHING FROM YOUR CHILDHOOD. CONSIDER WHAT THAT EVENT MEANT TO YOU AT THAT TIME, HOW IT HAS AFFECTED YOU TODAY, WHAT YOU CAN LEARN FROM IT, AND FINALLY, HOW IT CAN PREPARE YOU FOR THE FUTURE. UNDERSTANDING OUR PAST IS TO EMBRACE TRUE WISDOM.

Remember the days of old,
Consider the years of many
generations. Ask your father,
and he will show you; Your elders,
and they will tell you.

DEUTERONOMY 32:7

Cause me to hear Your lovingkindness in the morning, For in You do I trust; Cause me to know the way in which I should walk, For I lift up my soul to You.

PSALM 143:8

TAKE TIME TO

Take a Stroll

Most of us walk off and on throughout the day—to the car, out to the mailbox, through the grocery store, even for exercise. But how often do we *stroll?* It's not even a familiar word in contemporary vocabulary. Perhaps we consider strolling as something our grandparents did on a Sunday in the park. Actually, there's a definite art to strolling. To stroll, you must loosen your joints and slow down, breathe evenly, and observe the world around you as you go. It's an unhurried stride that heads nowhere in particular; but when you're done, you feel relaxed and refreshed.

ESTABLISH THE MINDSET TO TAKE A STROLL. REMEMBER, IT'S A SLOWED-DOWN WALK, CONTEMPLA- TIVE AND RELAXED. OBSERVE YOUR SURROUNDINGS AND ALLOW YOUR SOUL TO FOCUS ON GOD'S GOODNESS AS YOU MOVE ALONG AT A SERENE PACE.

Sincerely Compliment Someone

It's true—no one likes a schmoozer. But sometimes we're so careful not to dispense what might appear to be insincere flattery that we forget to offer admiration at all. This is unfortunate because everyone likes to be complimented from time to time—*especially* if it's sincere and from the heart. Of course, that's where it can become tricky. In order to give sincere compliments, we must sharpen our abilities to observe *and* to focus on the positive. When we do, however, we'll suddenly see others in a wonderful new light.

TAKE A MOMENT TO OBSERVE OTHERS AROUND YOU—COWORKERS, YOUR CHILDREN, YOUR SPOUSE, ETC. SEE IF YOU CAN CATCH THEM DOING SOMETHING GOOD, OR SIMPLY NOTICE A QUALITY YOU MAY HAVE PREVIOUSLY OVERLOOKED. THEN TELL THEM.

But exhort one another daily,
while it is called "Today," lest
any of you be hardened through
the deceitfulness of sin.

HEBREWS 3:13

Who redeems your life...Who crowns you with lovingkindness and tender mercies, Who satisfies your mouth with good things, So that your youth is renewed like the eagle's.

Psalm 103:4–5

Have a Facial or Manicure

We all want to be pampered once in a while, but our puritanical roots might make us think that such things are frivolous, selfish, extravagant, or simply a waste of time. Or maybe we think we're just not worth it. We forget that the way we care for and love ourselves usually translates into the way we care for and love others. By being stingy with ourselves, we often cheat others too. Remember that our Father in heaven loves to give good gifts to His children. Receive!

MAKE AN APPOINTMENT FOR A FACIAL, A MANICURE, OR SOME OTHER FORM OF PHYSICAL PAMPERING. THEN GO AND ALLOW YOURSELF TO FULLY ENJOY THE EXPERIENCE. REMEMBER THAT LOVING YOURSELF WILL HELP YOU TO LOVE OTHERS. RETURN REFRESHED.

TAKE TIME TO

Remember Someone Who is Gone

We all know someone who is no longer part of our lives—either through death or distance. We may have mourned this person's absence, then moved on. Or perhaps we're still unable to remember this person without experiencing fresh grief. But there comes a point of health when we can recall a loved one's memory and in essence celebrate their life. When we can remember how another has touched and changed us, then we can be truly grateful for their memory.

TAKE A MOMENT TO REMEMBER SOMEONE NO LONGER WITH YOU. INSTEAD OF FOCUSING ON THEIR ABSENCE, RECALL WAYS THAT THEIR WORDS OR ACTIONS CHANGED YOU FOR THE BETTER. EXPERIENCE GRATITUDE FOR THEM. CELEBRATE THE TIMES YOU SHARED.

When I was my father's son,
Tender and the only one in the sight
of my mother, He also taught me,
and said to me: "Let your heart
retain my words; Keep my
commands, and live."

PROVERBS 4:3–4

Be of good courage, And
He shall strengthen your heart,
All you who hope in the Lord.

PSALM 31:24

List Ten Things You Like about Yourself

Most of us can quickly rattle off everything we *don't* like about ourselves: the ways we need to change, the times we've failed, etc. Often we run this list through our minds, mentally chastising ourselves again and again. But how often do we focus on what we've done right, our accomplishments, our victories? While we know that focusing on the negative usually spawns more negativity, when it comes to our own lives, it's a hard habit to break. Yet, if "As [a man] thinks in his heart, so is he" (Prov. 23:7), can we retrain our minds to think differently?

TAKE A MOMENT TO LIST TEN THINGS ABOUT YOURSELF THAT YOU REALLY LIKE, THINGS LIKE PERSONALITY TRAITS, CHARACTER QUALITIES, SKILLS, GIFTS, ACCOMPLISHMENTS. THEN READ THE LIST OVER, SLOWLY FOCUSING ON EACH ONE. EXPRESS GRATITUDE TO GOD FOR HIS WORK IN YOUR LIFE.

TAKE TIME TO

Gaze at the Stars

Nothing spells out *eternity* quite like a clear, starry night. Gazing into the heavens, we come face to face with the majestic enormity of God—creator of heaven and earth—and the lover of our souls. Timeless stars, unfathomable distances, galaxies, light years… and God has it *all* in His hands. The constellations are like a giant, neon reader-board in the sky, reminding us who God is, and that He is in control. And yet how often we forget to stop and look up.

TAKE A MOMENT TO LOOK INTO THE NIGHT SKY. ENJOY THE PURE, SPARKLING BEAUTY. APPRECIATE THE BOUNDLESS MAGNITUDE. CELEBRATE THAT HE WHO MADE ALL THIS HAS ALSO MADE YOU. AND JUST AS HE COUNTS THE STARS, HE ALSO COUNTS EACH HAIR ON YOUR HEAD.

...I consider Your heavens,

the work of Your fingers,

The moon and the stars, which

You have ordained.

PSALM 8:3

"The wind blows where it wishes, and you hear the sound of it, but cannot tell where it comes from and where it goes. So is everyone who is born of the Spirit."

JOHN 3:8

TAKE TIME TO

Feel the Wind in Your Hair

We've all known a bad hair day, and it's something we don't usually welcome. But when was the last time you actually *felt* the sensation of the wind blowing through your hair? Did you turn up your collar and hunker down to avoid being mussed? Or did you simply relax and enjoy the liberating sensation of pure windblown abandonment? What a delight to embrace freedom when riding in a convertible with the top down, or with the car windows open, or walking outside in a brisk, autumn breeze.

Don't miss the next opportunity to feel the wind blow through your hair. Remember, hair can be restyled, but the pure sensation of freedom that comes with the wind can't be replicated. Welcome it with abandon!

Write a Love Note to God

We may realize it's important to communicate our love to God, but to write Him a letter? Where would we send it? Care of Saint Peter, the Pearly Gates of Heaven? The idea of writing a love note to God may seem strange at first, but as with many expressions, it might be more for us than Him. Taking the time to pen heartfelt words of love and appreciation to God create a link between our hearts and our heads. It reminds us of the depth of our love for Him. Whether we save the letter or burn it, the message will be received—both by God and us.

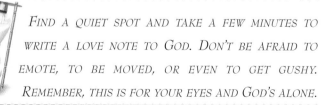

FIND A QUIET SPOT AND TAKE A FEW MINUTES TO WRITE A LOVE NOTE TO GOD. DON'T BE AFRAID TO EMOTE, TO BE MOVED, OR EVEN TO GET GUSHY. REMEMBER, THIS IS FOR YOUR EYES AND GOD'S ALONE.

"You shall love the LORD your God with all your heart, with all your soul, and with all your strength."

DEUTERONOMY 6:5

Wisdom is good with an inheritance, And profitable to those who see the sun. For wisdom is a defense as money is a defense, But the excellence of knowledge is that wisdom gives life to those who have it.

ECCLESIASTES 7:11–12

TAKE TIME TO
Look at Old Photos

Sometimes it's hard to look at old photos without taking a guilt trip for not having them all dated and mounted in a nice leather album. The fact is, many of us find it challenging to simply get our photos developed. Just the same, we shouldn't let misguided guilt distract us from the satisfaction of enjoying old photos. Every time we look at them we get a chance to see people and places from our past with a more mature set of eyes. We may notice things we overlooked before as we view the past from a broader perspective and increased wisdom.

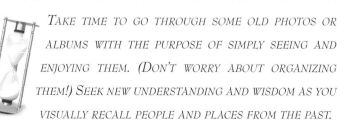

TAKE TIME TO GO THROUGH SOME OLD PHOTOS OR ALBUMS WITH THE PURPOSE OF SIMPLY SEEING AND ENJOYING THEM. (DON'T WORRY ABOUT ORGANIZING THEM!) SEEK NEW UNDERSTANDING AND WISDOM AS YOU VISUALLY RECALL PEOPLE AND PLACES FROM THE PAST.

TAKE TIME TO

Celebrate the Season

Life flows in cycles. The older we get, the faster they seem to go. And sometimes we hear ourselves dreading the change of seasons, despairing that summer must end, or that it's almost Christmas again. On the other hand, we can find comfort—a sense of order and well-being—in the recurrence of seasons. There is health to transitions: we need times to slow down and reflect as well as times to enjoy the sunshine. Seasonal changes provide us with those opportunities.

Take a moment to recognize the present season, whether it's coming or going, and then to welcome it. Try to see how the calendar season compares to the season of your soul. Is it time to harvest, time to bloom, time to rest? Celebrate the cycles of change that God brings into your world and your life!

"The LORD will open to you
His good treasure, the heavens,
to give the rain to your land in
its season, and to bless all the
work of your hand."

Deuteronomy 28:12

So that you incline your ear to wisdom, And apply your heart to understanding....If you seek her as silver, And search for her as for hidden treasures.

PROVERBS 2:2-4

Visit an Art Gallery

Even if you know absolutely nothing whatsoever about art, you're entitled to your opinions. Besides, "Beauty is in the eyes of the beholder." So don't use art "illiteracy" as an excuse not to visit a local gallery or exhibit. Something amazing always happens when we take time to examine and appraise the creativity of others. We begin to think and understand more creatively ourselves. We learn how to reason "outside of the box," and this kind of creativity can translate into many areas of our lives.

VISIT A LOCAL GALLERY OR ART EXHIBIT, ALLOWING YOURSELF ENOUGH TIME TO FULLY VIEW AND CONTEMPLATE THE WORKS. DON'T WORRY ABOUT HOW MUCH YOU KNOW OR DON'T KNOW ABOUT ART. CONSIDER HOW A CHILD MIGHT TAKE IT IN, AND GRANT YOURSELF THE SAME FREEDOM TO LIKE OR DISLIKE EACH INDIVIDUAL PIECE.

TAKE TIME TO

Praise Someone for an Accomplishment

Being mature and grown-up, we try to convince ourselves that we don't work to attain the appreciation of others. Still, who doesn't enjoy kudos or accolades once in awhile? Too often this type of praise is only bestowed when an accomplishment is obvious and grand. But what about the smaller accomplishments in life? Aren't they just as worthy of acknowledgment? Interestingly, an amazing by-product of praise is that when we pat someone else on the back, our spirits become lifted as well.

NOTICE SOMEONE AROUND YOU WHO HAS ACHIEVED SOMETHING BEYOND THE NORM. PERHAPS IT'S OBVIOUS, OR MAYBE IT'S OBSCURE. TAKE A FEW MOMENTS TO VERBALLY PRAISE, SEND A CONGRATULATORY E-MAIL, WRITE A THOUGHTFUL NOTE, OR DO WHATEVER SEEMS APPROPRIATE TO ACKNOWLEDGE THEIR ACCOMPLISHMENT.

And let us consider one another in order to stir up love and good works.

HEBREWS 10:2

Be anxious for nothing,
but in everything by prayer
and supplication, with
thanksgiving, let your requests be
made known to God.

Philippians 4:6

Give Your Cares to God

Sometimes we plod along day after day, and it feels as if we're carrying an unendurable load. We might actually experience physical soreness in our neck and shoulder muscles. Certainly the cares of this world aren't light, and they can become overwhelming. But God never expected us to carry these burdens alone; He didn't design us that way. However, He will not pry these cares from our grasp. He expects us to hand them over to Him so that He can bear them for us.

TAKE A MOMENT TO RECOGNIZE THE LOAD OF CARES THAT YOU MAY BE CARRYING. ACKNOWLEDGE THESE BURDENS TO GOD. THEN IMAGINE YOURSELF HANDING THESE WORRIES AND CARES OVER TO HIM. FINALLY, TRUST HIM TO CARRY THE LOAD FOR YOU.

TAKE TIME TO

Meditate on God's Goodness

Our minds can easily become preoccupied with life's daily demands: *Don't forget to stop by the cleaners. . . . Jenny needs new soccer shoes. . . . We're out of milk again. . . .* It may seem nearly impossible to slow these thought processes down. Even when we come before God, we might find ourselves running our laundry list of concerns past Him as well. When we learn to quiet our minds and come before Him thinking only of who He is and what He has done, our hearts are changed—and peace follows.

TAKE A MOMENT TO COME BEFORE GOD. CONSCIOUSLY EMPTY YOUR MIND OF THE CONCERNS OF THE DAY. PUT ASIDE ANY REQUESTS YOU WISH TO MAKE OF GOD. SIMPLY FOCUS ON HIS GOODNESS, HIS MAJESTY, HIS POWER, HIS WORKS, HIS GLORY. MEDITATE ON THESE ATTRIBUTES.

I will meditate on the glorious splendor of Your majesty, And on Your wondrous works.

PSALM 145:5

You are of God, little children...because He who is in you is greater than he who is in the world.

1 John 4:4

Go Barefoot

Do you remember the last time you went barefoot? Perhaps it was on a warm, sandy beach, or wading across an icy stream, or maybe it was way back in your childhood days. Do you recall the tingling sensation that came with each step? There's something deliciously earthy about the texture beneath an unshod foot. It's invigorating and refreshing—a wake-up call from a nearly forgotten childhood. It's something we need to experience more frequently.

LOOK FOR A MOMENT WHEN YOU CAN REMOVE YOUR SHOES AND SOCKS, BECOME CHILDLIKE, AND EXPERIENCE THE SENSATION OF GOING BAREFOOT. PERHAPS IT'S ONLY TO WALK ACROSS THE LAWN OR TO CURL YOUR TOES INTO THE NAP OF A NUBBY CARPET. WHATEVER THE OCCASION, RELISH THE EXPERIENCE, AND REMEMBER WHAT IT'S LIKE TO BE A CHILD.

Light a Candle

There is something almost spiritual about candle-light—the flickering, delicate, golden flame; the rich, translucent glow of warm wax; even the smell. It's no wonder Jesus so often spoke of light and lanterns: He knew our spirits would understand. Yet how often do we allow ourselves the enjoyment of candlelight? Why do we reserve this privilege for dinner parties or holidays? What was, in days gone past, a necessity, we now consider a luxury. Perhaps it's a luxury we can't afford to miss.

TAKE A MOMENT TO LIGHT A CANDLE (OR SEVERAL) FOR NO OTHER REASON THAN PURE, SIMPLE PLEASURE. DIM THE ELECTRIC LIGHTS AND OBSERVE THE WARM, COMFORTING GLOW. WATCH HOW THE CONTOURS OF A ROOM ARE SOFTENED BY CANDLELIGHT. RELAX AND ENJOY.

In Him was life, and the life was the light of men. And the light shines in the darkness, and the darkness did not comprehend it.

JOHN 1:4–5

Happy is the man who finds wisdom, And the man who gains understanding.

PROVERBS 3:13

TAKE TIME TO
Read a Good Novel

When was the last time you enjoyed a really good novel? Or do you consider reading fiction to be a waste of time? Have you ever considered that we sometimes learn about ourselves and others within the comfort zone of a fictional story? Some novels are meant to stretch us and expose us to people and places we might not otherwise experience. Others can relax, encourage, and refresh us. It's good to remember that Jesus taught some of His most powerful lessons by telling stories, otherwise known as parables.

TAKE TIME TO FIND A GOOD NOVEL. ASK FRIENDS FOR RECOMMENDATIONS, OR SIMPLY GO AND BROWSE. MAKE SURE YOU READ THE FIRST FEW PAGES BEFORE MAKING A SELECTION. THEN ALLOW YOURSELF TO BECOME LOST IN THE STORY. FIND THE LESSONS TO BE GLEANED THERE.

TAKE TIME TO

Plant Something

As children, we weren't usually worried about dirtying our hands. We dug holes, made mud pies, planted marigold seeds. Yet as we grew older, we may have grown increasingly suspicious of dirt, keeping a safe distance lest we become soiled. But there is something unexplainably soothing and earth-connecting about sinking your fingers into good, soft soil. Whether it's planting sunflower seeds or tulip bulbs, or transplanting an indoor ivy plant, the process is incredibly rewarding. Besides, fingernails can be scrubbed!

BEFORE PLANTING, CONSIDER THE SEASON. (BULBS OUT-SIDE IN THE FALL; SEEDS OR PERENNIALS IN THE SPRING; FORCED BULBS INSIDE IN THE WINTER; REPOT A HOUSEPLANT ANYTIME.) GATHER APPROPRIATE TOOLS, THEN ENJOY THE SENSATION OF EARTH BETWEEN YOUR FINGERS AS YOU PLANT.

And the earth brought forth grass,
the herb that yields seed....and the
tree that yields fruit....And God
saw that it was good.

GENESIS 1:12

"Take heed that you do not despise one of these little ones, for...their angels always see the face of My Father who is in heaven."

MATTHEW 18:10

TAKE TIME TO
Hold a Baby

For those of us who've reared children, we sometimes forget how relieved we were to let someone
else hold our baby while we had a little break.
Perhaps, in our exhausted state of young mother-
hood, we didn't realize the priceless gift we were
sharing by handing over our infant. To look into a
baby's placid eyes is to catch a glance at eternity—a
tiny peek into heaven. The innocence, the trust, the
purity—nothing else on earth quite captures these
qualities like babyhood.

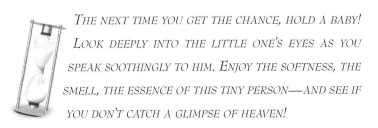

*THE NEXT TIME YOU GET THE CHANCE, HOLD A BABY!
LOOK DEEPLY INTO THE LITTLE ONE'S EYES AS YOU
SPEAK SOOTHINGLY TO HIM. ENJOY THE SOFTNESS, THE
SMELL, THE ESSENCE OF THIS TINY PERSON—AND SEE IF
YOU DON'T CATCH A GLIMPSE OF HEAVEN!*

Organize a Drawer

No one likes to live in a state of chaos, but sometimes schedules are so demanding that it's hard to make time to restore order. Perhaps the mere idea of organizing *anything* sounds like work, or for some of us, torture. But a small and contained organizational task can prove very refreshing when thoughtfully done. It brings a soothing sense of control and peace into our lives. The first thing to remember is to *not* get carried away. Limit yourself to one small project—like a drawer.

TAKE TIME TO SELECT A DRAWER (A PERSONAL ONE FOR STARTERS, LIKE YOUR DESK, LINGERIE, OR TOILETRIES DRAWER). THEN CAREFULLY SORT, DISPOSE, AND ORGANIZE. PERHAPS USE DIVIDERS, A NEW DRAWER LINER, OR A FRAGRANT SACHET. THEN STEP BACK AND APPRECIATE HOW YOU'VE RESTORED ORDER OUT OF CHAOS.

The steps of a good
man are ordered by
the LORD, And
He delights
in his way.

PSALM 37:23

Let me have joy . . .
refresh my heart in the Lord.

PHILEMON 20

Take a Minivacation

Some companies grant special time off called a "mental health day." Not all of us, however, get to enjoy such corporate benefits. Still, if we try, we might discover a way to give ourselves a day off—a time when we can take a "minivacation." But we must guard against filling this day with the normal demands of everyday living. The way we prevent this is to *take ourselves away* for the duration of the day. We give ourselves a much-needed break of relaxation and refreshment so we can return invigorated and ready to face life's challenges once again.

GIVE YOURSELF THE DAY OFF. PLAN TO GO AND SEE AND DO WHATEVER IT IS THAT YOU NEVER SEEM TO HAVE TIME FOR. BUT MAKE SURE THAT YOU CHOOSE ACTIVITIES THAT ARE BOTH REFRESHING AND STIMULATING.

TAKE TIME TO

Attend a Concert

Many of us often enjoy a new CD or a good stereo system, but what can compare to a live concert in a wonderful setting? There's something amazingly energizing about hearing live musicians, with finely tuned instruments or beautiful voices, performing before a crowd of enthusiastic fans. Whether you experience a full orchestra in a beautiful concert hall, a jazz festival by the lake, or a bell choir in a country church—the results can be inconceivable. It can change your heart.

PLAN TO TAKE IN A LIVE MUSICAL EVENT. LEAVE HOME EARLY SO THAT YOU DON'T FEEL RUSHED. TAKE TIME TO ENJOY THE AMBIENCE OF MUSICIANS WARMING UP, THE ENERGY OF THE CROWD, AND THE CHARACTERISTICS OF THE SETTING. THEN SIT BACK AND ENJOY!

Then David and all the
house of Israel played music
before the LORD on all
kinds of instruments.

2 SAMUEL 6:5

Conclusion

As we learn to slow down and *take time* for the things that are truly important in life, we find we are changed—*transformed* even! We become more relaxed—more at ease with ourselves and our environment—and even our countenance softens. For we begin to view the world differently, and we pay attention to things we might have otherwise overlooked. When we learn to take time, we find our lives are remarkably enriched.

So perhaps we need to take a moment to share what we've learned with others. To give them the "gift of time" so that they might experience the wonder and appreciation of a life well-lived themselves. What a wonderful world it would be if we could all learn to "take time."

About the Author

Melody Carlson is an award-winning author of over forty books for children, teens, and adults. She writes full-time from her "little cabin in the wood" in the beautiful Cascade Mountains of Oregon. However, life wasn't always so tranquil and serene—she spent many years working hard, mothering two boys now grown, and running too fast—but is thankful to be living a quieter and fuller life now, and she believes that "simple pleasures are truly the best." When not writing, she enjoys gardening and reading, biking and hiking with her husband, skiing with her sons, and walking her chocolate lab, Bailey, in the woods. Her goal in writing is to be used by God to touch readers, of all ages, in memorable and life-changing ways. Other titles by Melody include: the Whispering Pine Series; the Allison Chronicles, *Homeward, King of the Stable,* and *The Wonder of Christmas.*